D1736623

WEATHER MYTHS,
BUSTED!

by Carol Hand

www.12StoryLibrary.com

12-Story Library is an imprint of Peterson Publishing Company and Press Room Editions.

Produced for 12-Story Library by Red Line Editorial

Photographs ©: Stefano Garau/Shutterstock Images, cover, 1, 8; MidoSemsem/Shutterstock Images, 4; Gyorgy Barna/Shutterstock Images, 5; swisoot/Shutterstock Images, 6; alexsvirid/Shutterstock Images, 7; Marcel Jancovic/Shutterstock Images, 9; De Visu/Shutterstock Images, 10; Miriam Doerr/Shutterstock Images, 11; Arthur Rothstein/FSA/OWI Collection/Library of Congress, 12; oticki/iStockphoto/Thinkstock, 13; potenciaverde/iStockphoto/Thinkstock, 14; Fred Driscoll/Library of Congress, 15; Nick Krug/The Lawrence Journal-World/AP Images, 16; Minerva Studio/Shutterstock Images, 18, 29; Brian A Jackson/Shutterstock Images, 20; NASA, 21, 24; John Vachon/FSA/OWI Collection/Library of Congress, 22; Meg Wallace Photography/Shutterstock Images, 23, 28; Alexey Stiop/Shutterstock Images, 26; Ann Johansson/Corbis, 27

Library of Congress Cataloging-in-Publication Data
Cataloging-in-publication information is on file with the Library of Congress.
978-1-63235-307-8 (hardcover)
978-1-63235-357-3 (paperback)
978-1-62143-472-6 (hosted ebook)

Printed in the United States of America
Mankato, MN
May, 2016

Access free, up-to-date content on this topic plus a full digital version of this book. Scan the QR code on page 31 or use your school's login at 12StoryLibrary.com.

Table of Contents

Busted: Four Elements Are Responsible for Weather

Early weather watchers did not know what caused weather. They could not predict it. But that did not stop them from writing about it. The Greek scientist Aristotle wrote four books on weather. He lived more than 2,300 years ago. Aristotle was very intelligent. But much of his science was wrong. Aristotle did not test his ideas. He only thought about them. He did not measure or do experiments.

SEASONS

Aristotle also thought stars and planets orbited Earth. In 1543, Nicolaus Copernicus proved Aristotle was wrong. Copernicus showed Earth orbited the Sun. This discovery helped explain why seasons changed. As Earth orbits the Sun, it rotates on its axis. But this axis is tilted. The tilt changes the angle at which the sun's rays hit the earth. This causes the change in seasons. Aristotle's theory could not explain seasons.

Aristotle thought only four elements made up all matter on Earth. These were earth, air, fire, and water. He thought these elements worked together to cause weather.

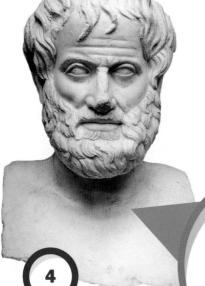

Aristotle came up with the four elements theory but never tested it.

A barometer records atmospheric pressure.

Aristotle believed the sun caused large masses of air to move. He thought water vapor formed clouds. These statements happen to be true. But the four elements could not explain most weather.

Starting in the fifteenth century, scientists began to make instruments to measure weather changes. They made instruments to measure humidity, temperature, and air pressure. Now, they could begin to understand weather. They started to understand that many factors affected weather.

2,000
Number of years people accepted Aristotle's ideas.

- Aristotle claimed four elements controlled weather: earth, air, fire, and water.
- His ideas did not explain most weather.
- In the fifteenth century, scientists began to invent instruments to measure weather changes.

THINK ABOUT IT

Science has changed a lot since Aristotle's time. Explain what changes have occurred to cause people to turn away from most of Aristotle's science.

Busted: Celsius Tops Fahrenheit in Temperature Measurement

Early inventors made simple thermometers. But these thermometers all had different scales. You could not compare their temperatures.

Daniel Gabriel Fahrenheit was a German instrument maker. In 1724, he made a temperature scale everyone could use. First, he created the 0° mark for his scale. To do so, he used the temperature of a mixture of ice and sea salt. On this scale, the freezing point of water became 30°. Fahrenheit's body temperature measurement was 90°. Later, he added the boiling point of water (212°). He also changed the melting point of water from 30° to 32°. He adjusted

the body temperature measurement to 98.6°.

Fahrenheit's temperature scale was accurate. But it was a little confusing. In 1742, Swedish astronomer Anders Celsius created a simpler scale. He defined the freezing point of water as 0°.

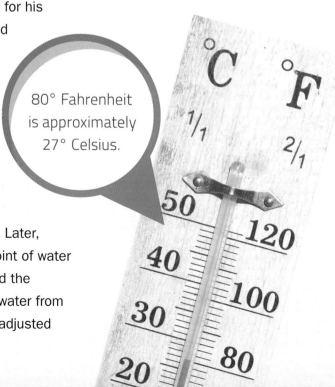

80° Fahrenheit is approximately 27° Celsius.

A cricket's chirp gets slower as the temperature drops.

The boiling point of water was 100°. These rounded measurements were easier to understand than Fahrenheit's odd-numbered ones. This simple scale is the Celsius scale.

People still use the scales developed by Fahrenheit and Celsius. Nearly every country in the world uses the Celsius scale. The United States uses the Fahrenheit scale.

37
Temperature of the human body in degrees Celsius.

- Before Fahrenheit, temperatures on different thermometers could not be compared.
- Fahrenheit's temperature scale goes from 0° to 212°; ice melts at 32°, and water boils at 212°.
- In the Celsius scale, the low of 0° represents the freezing point of water and the high of 100° the boiling point of water.

TEMPERATURE BY CRICKET

Crickets' temperatures are the same as the air temperature. In hot weather, crickets chirp rapidly. In cold weather, their chirps slow down. Use a stopwatch to measure the number of chirps in 15 seconds. Add 37 to get the approximate temperature in degrees Fahrenheit. This temperature might not be exact, but it will be close.

Busted: Hot Weather Causes Heat Lightning

On hot summer nights, it is common to see lightning light the sky. But often, no clap of thunder follows it. People call this heat lightning. Heat lightning is far away, so we do not hear its thunder. It usually happens in summer. Many people think hot weather causes it. But it is just normal lightning from a distant thunderstorm.

When you slide across a carpet and touch something metal, you get a shock. This is static electricity. It happens when opposite electrical charges meet. Static electricity inside storm clouds causes lightning. Lightning heats the air five times hotter than the sun. The air swells, causing a tremendous explosion: thunder.

Thunder always follows lightning but people might not hear it.

It is possible to see lightning right away. But sound travels much more slowly than light. It also does not travel as far. Even if we see lightning, thunder may disappear before we hear it. We can see lightning from 100 miles (160 km) away. But we usually cannot hear thunder more than 10 miles (16 km) away. Mountains also can block the sound of thunder. Sound waves in thunderstorms bend up toward the sky rather than down to the ground. If the sound waves do not bounce off Earth, humans will not hear thunder.

The static electricity causing this toddler's hair to stand on end also causes lightning.

THINK ABOUT IT

Thunder accompanies heat lightning, but humans often cannot hear it. How do scientists know it still occurs? Use evidence from the text to support your answer.

5
Seconds it takes thunder to travel 1 mile (1.6 km).

- Heat lightning is from thunderstorms so far away the thunder is not heard.
- Lightning results from static electricity in clouds.
- Sound travels more slowly than light, so we can see but not hear a faraway storm.

9

Busted: Heat Waves Are Impossible to Predict

Heat waves are the most deadly weather events in the United States. They kill more people each year than tornadoes, floods, earthquakes, and hurricanes put together. In summer 2012, 8,000 US high-temperature records were broken or tied. It was so hot in some regions, the pavement buckled. Many people lost their lives.

There is nothing scientists can do to stop a heat wave. And until 2013, many scientists believed predicting heat waves was also an impossible task. Forecasters were able to forecast heat waves up to 10 days in advance. But more lives could be saved if meteorologists could give more advance warning.

In 2013, scientists made a breakthrough at the US National Center for Atmospheric Research. They used a model to simulate the past 12,000 years of weather. Within those years, the United States

People seek relief from a heat wave in Moscow, Russia, in 2015.

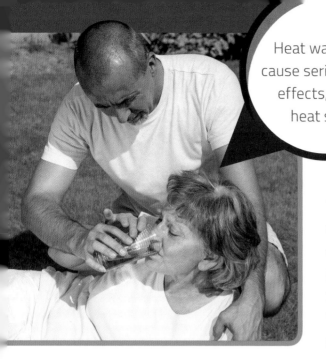

Heat waves may cause serious health effects, such as heat stroke.

experienced 5,900 heat waves. That was enough to look for patterns.

The researchers found a particular set of pressure patterns that often came before heat waves. The pressure patterns occurred 15 to 20 days before a heat wave would. The sequence did not occur before all heat waves. But researchers are confident their findings will lead to more accurate future forecasts.

STAYING COOL IN A HEAT WAVE

Heat waves are deadly, but many people do not take them seriously. No homes are destroyed. There are no dramatic storm images. But heat waves do cause severe harm. It is possible to avoid a heat-related illness. Dress in lightweight and light-colored clothing. Drink lots of water and avoid meat. The body produces more heat to break down meat and other protein. Stay in the air conditioning and out of the sun as much as possible.

50,000
Number of people who died during a heat wave in Europe in 2003.

- Heat waves are the deadliest weather events.
- Scientists have been able to forecast heat waves only up to 10 days in advance.
- Now, new research may make it possible to forecast a heat wave more than 10 days away.

5

Busted: Rain "Follows the Plow"

In the nineteenth century, many people settled in Midwest states such as Nebraska, Kansas, and Oklahoma. They plowed prairie grasses and planted wheat and corn. Some people thought plowed soil would act like a sponge and soak up rainfall. The extra water would go into the air as vapor and fall as rain. That is, rain would "follow the plow."

A University of Nebraska scientist wrote about this idea. He thought plowing would increase rainfall. He believed farmers could stop irrigating farmland. It was easy to believe this when

Poor farming practices and drought caused Midwestern farms to turn to dust.

it rained. But there was almost no rain from 1887 to 1897. This drought, plus too much plowing, caused loss of soil. Rainfall

Today, farmers consult the weather forecast, not the plow, for signs of rain.

remained low. Fifty years later, in the 1930s, the Midwest had become the Dust Bowl. Farmland was ruined. Millions of people left the Midwest. It took many years to renew the soil.

Soil loss and drought combine to damage farmland. But can agriculture really affect weather? Some scientists today think it might have local effects. Planting crops might be cooling the Midwest. Corn crops might change the temperature at which dew forms. This can lead to more severe thunderstorms.

30.25
Inches (496 mL) of average annual rainfall in Nebraska.

- Rain "follows the plow" meant that plowing prairies would increase rainfall.
- People believed this idea during the mid- and late nineteenth century.
- A major drought from 1887 to 1897 showed that plowing caused soil loss, not more rain.

Busted: The Cosmos Cause the Weather

Before computer models, ancient weather watchers looked to the stars to predict the weather. They believed the moon, sun, planets, and stars determined the weather on Earth. The position of these celestial bodies in relation to one another influenced Earth's weather.

The early weather astrologers believed the moon controlled rainfall. Two full moons in one month was thought to send floods. A pale full moon predicted rain. The days surrounding a new or full moon were stormy.

In 1671, Scottish astrologer William Cock wrote a book on forecasting. He outlined different cosmic factors that determined weather. He said the nature and movement of the planets predicted the weather. So did the different signs of the zodiac. Comets and eclipses could make Earth's weather change.

Scientists continued to believe the cosmos

A pale full moon was thought to predict rain.

By 1943, meteorologists were using computers to forecast weather.

caused Earth's weather. But that assumption started to change in the eighteenth century. Wealthy people set up weather stations at their homes. They measured temperature, wind, rain, and pressure. By the mid-nineteenth century, many became skeptical of the astrologic forecasts. But they still did not know how to use their data to predict the weather. Accurate predictions would not become available until the invention of computers in the 1950s.

12
Cosmic factors astrologer William Cock believed affected Earth's weather.

- Ancient weather watchers believed the planets, Moon, and Sun determined Earth's weather.
- Astrologer William Cock wrote a book outlining the planets' effect on weather.
- People started gathering weather data in the eighteenth century, but scientists were not able to make accurate predictions until the 1950s.

15

Busted: Past Weather Can Predict Today's Weather

In the nineteenth century, scientists improved weather instruments. They began to keep better records. In 1837, Samuel Morse invented the telegraph. It helped scientists communicate around the globe. Meteorologists shared their weather observations. They set up weather stations. They made simple weather maps. Some meteorologists predicted weather by comparing past weather patterns with present ones. But this method did not give accurate weather forecasts.

Lewis Fry Richardson was a British physicist during the early twentieth century. He wanted to improve weather forecasting.

Meteorologist Gordon Strassberg attaches a radiosonde to a weather balloon in Kansas in 2006.

RADIOSONDES AND WEATHER PREDICTION

The radiosonde was invented in the 1920s. It is a small, lightweight box. It is filled with weather instruments and a radio. Scientists attach it to a balloon and send it high into the atmosphere. Its instruments send readings to a station on the ground. The readings help predict weather. Today, scientists send up radiosondes every 12 hours from stations around the world.

Richardson chose not to use past weather to create his predictions. Instead, he used a mathematical model. A model is a simple copy of a system. In 1910, Richardson designed a mathematical model of Earth's atmosphere. Richardson included data for temperature, wind speed, and other weather measurements.

Richardson spent weeks building his first forecast. He did the math with pencil and paper. Doing the math this way took far too long.

6
Number of weeks Richardson needed to forecast a change in air pressure over a six-hour period.

- Early weather predictions inaccurately compared past weather with present weather.
- Lewis Fry Richardson was the first scientist to use math to figure a weather forecast.
- Though it took too long to compute to be useful in his lifetime, his mathematical model is the basis of today's computing forecasting models.

Richardson's methods were not practical. To get quick forecasts, thousands of people would have to work together. Engineers built the first computers in the 1950s. Richardson's mathematical forecasting was finally possible. Meteorologists still use his method today. However, today's models are bigger, faster, and more complete.

Busted: Tornadoes and Hurricanes Strike Without Warning

Before weather forecasts, tornadoes and hurricanes seemed to strike without warning. Or, that is what people believed happened. In the twentieth century, a number of technologies helped bust this myth. Scientists developed tools to predict when tornadoes and hurricanes were coming.

A tornado is a powerful wind storm. Its rotating winds can be powerful enough to destroy buildings. The first tornado forecast in the United States occurred on March 20, 1948. It was made available to an Oklahoma Air Force weather office. The forecast warned weather conditions might cause tornadoes. Six hours later, a tornado struck the Air Force base. No base personnel were killed because they had heard the forecast. They took shelter from the storm.

In 1953, the US Weather Bureau formed a center for severe storm warnings. Weather forecasters began to use radar to locate storms. Radar

Tornadoes are fast-forming and devastating storms.

let the forecasters see storms and observe their direction and speed. The forecasters could give tornado warnings approximately five minutes before a tornado struck. In the 1990s, scientists developed an improved radar system called Doppler. Now, people have 10 to 13 minutes of warning before a tornado hits. But scientists still cannot tell exactly where a tornado will touch down.

A hurricane is a huge, swirling windstorm that begins over an ocean. Hurricane warnings began in the 1930s, but prediction was difficult. In 1975, the National Aeronautics and Space Administration (NASA) launched a satellite to track hurricanes. The data allowed meteorologists to make accurate predictions and issue warnings. The early warnings saved many lives. Radar and computer models helped forecasters learn a hurricane's direction and strength. In 2015, meteorologists could give five-day forecasts.

7

Number of days between the formation and landfall of Hurricane Sandy on the US East Coast in 2012.

- Before radar, there was no way to predict storms.
- Radar gives forecasters the location, direction, and speed of a storm.
- Satellites and computer models also help in storm prediction.

Busted: Raindrops Are Teardrop-Shaped

Most people think raindrops are teardrop-shaped, with a wide, rounded bottom and a pointed top. Drawings of raindrops in books or magazines look like this. Even forecasters use this shape to show rain on weather maps. But a raindrop is not shaped like a tear. Its shape changes with time.

Raindrops begin high in the atmosphere. Water collects around tiny bits of smoke or dust. Here, the tiny raindrops are approximately 0.04 inch (1 mm) across. They are round

> Raindrops change shape as they fall.

0.18
Diameter, in inches (4.5 mm), a raindrop can reach before it falls apart.

- Raindrops are not teardrop shaped.
- Tiny raindrops are round because of surface tension.
- As raindrops fall and get larger, they flatten due to air pressure.

because of surface tension. The surface tension acts like a skin. It holds the water together.

As a raindrop falls through the atmosphere, its speed increases. Air pushes up on it from below. This makes the raindrop flatten on the bottom. Sometimes, it bumps into another raindrop and gets bigger. It starts to look like the top half of a hamburger bun. The raindrop continues to flatten. At some point, it will get too big. It will change shape again. This time, it will look like a parachute with bags of water on each side. Then, it will fall apart into smaller drops.

1.

2.

3.

4.

5.

6.

A NASA study shows how two raindrops become one.

Scientists from NASA study the shape of rain. The shape of the rain helps them figure out the next hour's weather. The shapes tell them if a storm is getting stronger or weaker. It helps them handle storm emergencies. They can even help guide airplanes to land safely. The shape of rain is an important weather tool. But raindrops are never shaped like teardrops.

THINK ABOUT IT

Many weather forecast maps portray rain as teardrops. Should weather forecasters change the shape of rain on weather maps? Would a more accurate shape make it easier for people to understand the forecast? Why or why not?

Busted: Mild, Cloudy Days Cause Blizzards

On January 12, 1888, a severe blizzard hit the Midwest. The weather started out mild and cloudy. But then it changed drastically. The temperature in Minnesota dropped to −53.5° Fahrenheit (−47.5°C) in 11 hours. The wind blew up to 48 miles per hour (77 km/h). The blizzard raged across six states. It killed 235 people, including many children. Some children were caught in their one-room schoolhouses. Others were lost trying to get home through the blizzard. People called the storm the "Children's Blizzard."

A few years later, a man from South Dakota wrote an article for a weather magazine. He claimed blizzards always came on days that

It was a mild January day before the Children's Blizzard hit.

34.5

Record number of inches (87.6 cm) of snow a single blizzard dumped on Worcester, Massachusetts, in January 2015.

- In 1888, a deadly Midwestern blizzard started on a mild, cloudy day.
- People believed mild, cloudy weather meant that a blizzard was coming.
- Today, scientists know blizzards occur with the appropriate combination of cold air, moisture, and lift.

> Today, forecasters can inform the public about a major storm before it hits.

began mild and cloudy. This had happened on the day of the Children's Blizzard. He said schools should stay closed on these days and people should stay home. But it turns out this idea is not an effective way to forecast a blizzard.

Mild temperatures and cloudy skies cannot predict a blizzard. Cold air, moisture, and lift cause a blizzard to occur. The air must be below freezing to make snow rather than rain. Moisture to make clouds and snow often blows in from an ocean or lake. Lift raises the moist air up to form clouds and snow. Today's weather forecasters can recognize these conditions. They can tell when a blizzard is coming.

Busted: Cloud Movement Drives Hurricanes

Scientists once thought groups of storm clouds over the ocean could release more energy than scattered clouds could release. They thought this energy formed hurricanes. Scientists called this theory convection. Convection is the vertical movement of energy when warm air rises and cool air sinks. The theory says storm clouds clump together and generate energy. This makes them move in a circular path. Convection is a factor in

The eye of Hurricane Earl in 2011 was 17 miles (28 km) across.

TYPHOON HAIYAN

Hurricanes are called typhoons when they occur in the Pacific Ocean. The most powerful typhoon to ever make landfall struck in November 2013. Typhoon Haiyan hit the Philippines with winds up to 195 miles per hour (313.8 km/h). It destroyed coastal cities, wiping out homes and killing more than 7,000 people.

hurricane formation. But it does not tell the whole story.

Hurricanes do not just start anywhere there is a group of clouds over the ocean. Today, scientists know hurricanes begin in the tropics. Warm, moist air at the ocean surface pushes cooler air up into the atmosphere. As warm air rises, it cools to form rain and storm clouds. Strong winds high in the atmosphere push against the rising air. The winds move the warmer air away from the storm's center. This movement, plus Earth's rotation, pushes the wind in a circle. The spinning wind has a calm "eye" in the center. A hurricane has started.

Hurricanes are formed when warm air at the ocean surface meets cooler air higher up. Hurricanes grow stronger as long as they can collect warm, moist air and move it upward.

Convection explains how the air moves. But it does not fully explain how hurricanes are created.

190
Wind speed, in miles per hour (305.8 km/h), of the strongest hurricane to hit the United States, Hurricane Camille in 1969.

- Scientists once thought convection was the sole cause of hurricanes.
- Hurricanes form when warm, moist air at the ocean surface rises to meet cooler air in the atmosphere.
- Hurricanes build energy as long as there is warm, moist ocean air to fuel them.

Busted: Open Windows During a Tornado

Tornadoes are smaller storms than hurricanes. But they have much stronger winds. Strong tornadoes can destroy everything in their paths. Over the years, scientists have recommended many ways to stay safe during a tornado. Today, scientists know not all of these ways are effective.

Scientists once thought closed windows would cause a house to explode. The closed windows would create different pressures inside and outside a house. They told homeowners to open windows during a tornado. Doing so, they said, would make inside and outside

A strong tornado's winds are devastating whether windows are open or closed.

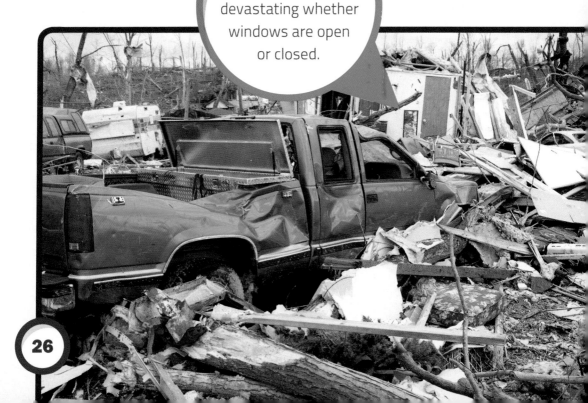

pressures equal. This would prevent an explosion.

Today, scientists know better. A tornado's winds are very, very strong. They break windows. Once they do, winds can push up on the roof and tear it off. The same thing may happen through an open window. An open window can put people at risk. Flying glass and debris may hit them.

Now, scientists recommend people leave windows closed. They should find shelter away from windows, doors, and exterior walls. Basements and inside rooms are the safest places to be in a tornado. A blanket, sleeping bag, or mattress can protect people from flying debris.

Basements and interior rooms with no windows are the safest places to be during a tornado.

318
Approximate wind speed, in miles per hour (511.8 km/h), of the strongest tornado ever recorded.

- Tornadoes are smaller than hurricanes but have stronger winds.
- Opening windows during a tornado is not helpful or safe.
- Instead, leave windows closed and seek shelter in the basement or an inside room.

Fact Sheet

- Scientists began to better understand weather when they made instruments to measure it. Weather instruments include thermometers (to measure temperature), hygrometers (to measure humidity), anemometers (to measure wind speed), and barometers (to measure air pressure).

- Lightning happens when positive and negative electrical charges in clouds crash into each other, building up static electricity. When negative charges in clouds get near the ground, they attract positive charges on the ground. This causes cloud-to-ground lightning, which can strike people and objects on the ground. Lightning occurs with severe storms, especially thunderstorms and tornadoes. The best way to stay safe from lightning is to stay indoors.

- Lewis Fry Richardson pioneered the use of mathematics in weather forecasting. He was one of many scientists of his time who began to apply math to fields of science that had not used it before. This made weather and other sciences much more precise. Richardson tried to describe weather using equations, or mathematical statements. He put numbers for temperature, wind speed, and other weather measurements into these statements.

- Radar and satellites made forecasts much more accurate. Forecasters could see storms developing. They could tell a storm's size, speed, and direction. They could provide warnings before it hit. Predictions improved as instruments improved. Warnings happened sooner. Storms still cause damage. But now, people are better prepared, and fewer people are killed.

- Most people think severe storms such as tornadoes and hurricanes are the most deadly weather events. But heat waves killed more people in the United States between 2003 and 2013 than any other weather event. Heat killed 1,340 people in the United States during that 10-year period. Tornadoes killed 1,145; hurricanes killed 1,143; and floods killed 806.

Glossary

astrologer
Someone who predicts the weather and other events by interpreting the stars and planets.

cosmos
The universe.

drought
A period of very low or no rainfall, causing water shortages.

humidity
The amount of moisture, or water, in the air.

hurricane warning
An official weather alert that means a hurricane is expected within a certain area.

irrigating
Supplying with water.

mathematical model
A copy of a real-life process, such as weather, that uses math to predict that process's future behavior.

radar
Device that locates objects using radio waves.

static electricity
Electricity that collects on the surfaces of objects and builds up in one place.

tornado warning
An official weather alert that means a tornado is occurring or could occur within a certain area.

For More Information

Books

Furgang, Kathy. *Everything Weather: Facts, Photos, and Fun That Will Blow Your Mind!* Washington, DC: National Geographic, 2012.

Kostigen, Thomas. *Extreme Weather: Surviving Tornadoes, Sandstorms, Hailstorms, Blizzards, Hurricanes, and More!* Washington, DC: National Geographic, 2014.

Krohn, Katherine. *The Whirlwind World of Hurricanes with Max Axiom, Super Scientist.* Mankato, MN: Capstone Press, 2011.

Visit 12StoryLibrary.com

Scan the code or use your school's login at **12StoryLibrary.com** for recent updates about this topic and a full digital version of this book. Enjoy free access to:

- Digital ebook
- Breaking news updates
- Live content feeds
- Videos, interactive maps, and graphics
- Additional web resources

Note to educators: Visit 12StoryLibrary.com/register to sign up for free premium website access. Enjoy live content plus a full digital version of every 12-Story Library book you own for every student at your school.

Index

About the Author

Carol Hand is a science writer specializing in earth and life science. She has written approximately 30 nonfiction books on various topics, including weather and climate change.

READ MORE FROM 12-STORY LIBRARY

Every 12-Story Library book is available in many formats. For more information, visit 12StoryLibrary.com.